HOW TO TYPE FAST
SAVE TIME, BOOST PRODUCTIVITY, AND DOUBLE YOUR TYPING SPEED

BRANDON NANKIVELL

TABLE OF CONTENTS

WHY YOU SHOULD READ THIS BOOK

The aim of this book is to help you become more productive and save time by helping you learn to type faster. Most guides out there leave out valuable information and often focus merely on a technique called touch typing. Of the few typing books on the Kindle store that I paid for, I was disappointed to be presented with scrappy information and less than 500 words. As a typing enthusiast, I wrote this book because I believe there was potential for higher quality guides to help you become a super-fast typist in order to save you time, boost your productivity, and potentially triple your typing speed. This guide has been carefully crafted to make sure you are aware of the awesome benefits you'll receive and exactly how to obtain them. Once you learn to type fast, you'll never look back. Whether you're a student, an office administrator, an online gamer, a writer, a computer programmer, or even unemployed, there is value in this book for you no matter how fast you can type. How do people type so fast? What is the best way to type? Does it matter what keyboard I use? How can I benefit from typing fast? Are there any other good typing tips besides 'practice'? How long will it take me to learn how to type fast? These are questions you may be asking yourself, and I'm here to answer them for you. In this book, you'll learn how to set a well-defined goal that will bring you closer to being a fast and fluent typist. I'll explain what ergonomics is and how to apply it (this is the boring part, but I highly recommend you pay attention as this affects not just your health, but your typing speed as well!). Next you'll learn what different keyboards there are and how they affect typing. You'll be surprised at how many different kinds of keyboards there are and why you can benefit from selecting the right one. With your new realization of just how much typing has the capacity to enhance your life, you'll be eager to know how to touch type if you don't already. If you do, this chapter is still worth a read to brush up your technique, considering its lays the foundation for typing effectively and efficiently as fast as possible. I'll explain what it is and how to do it, without all the technical jargon. I have compiled a list of the 35 most valuable typing tips I've come across based on personal experience and the experiences of numerous top typists around the globe. You won't find another list like this on the web of such quantity and quality. At the end of the book will be a list of action steps that you can take and 3 bonus chapters. Finally, the book will conclude with a list answers to the questions I get asked most. Although this book aims to answer all your questions, if you have a more personalized one, feel free to ask it on the TypeGood website or Facebook page and I'll be happy to help. I've also included ways to make money by typing, and a case study that takes you on an inside journey of how I went from typing 0 wpm to averaging 125 wpm and frequently hitting higher speeds up to 150 wpm using the concepts in this book.

The Benefits of Typing Fast

The benefits of touch typing fast are overlooked. Imagine being able to spend more time on things you love, instead of being stuck with your head down trying to look for the right keys. After reading the benefits below, you'll begin to understand why it will change your life.

Increased productivity

Considering the average person types 40 wpm, if you typed a document at a rate of 120 wpm, you would finish it 3 times faster than the average person! Whether you're a student at college, an employee, or a writer - this will free up time for more important tasks.

Save time

Time is your most valuable asset. By learning to touch type, you no longer need to look down at the keyboard. This allows you to focus and save time. Assuming you can type 120 wpm and type 10,000 words a week, you would save almost 3 hours per week or 156 hours per year.

Impress your friends, family, co-workers, and your boss

As you mash away on the keyboard, you are likely to attract attention from your peers.

STANDOUT TO EMPLOYERS

These days employers seek those with computer skills and being able to type fast comes under that umbrella. Some professions require a minimum typing speed such as legal writers and police officers.

ELIMINATE FATIGUE AND FEEL GOOD

After long periods of typing your neck, hands, and back begin to tire. By following the correct touch typing technique, you can eliminate this. You will no longer have to crane your neck to look down at the keyboard. Additionally, it's less mental effort to switch your focus between the screen and keyboard, allowing you to get more done in less time.

ENHANCE COMMUNICATION

Whether you play online games or message on social media, being able to type faster will make you highly responsive in less time. This can be advantageous in online games where you don't have much time to type in between certain scenarios, but you need to talk to your teammates. If you're on social media, your peers will appreciate lightning-fast responses!

TAKE BETTER NOTES

Typing fast allows you to take more notes as someone is speaking. The average rate of speech is 120-150 wpm so if you can type the same speed, you can record everything they say! Remember more thanks to your typing skills.

TYPE OVER 100 WORDS PER MINUTE

Exceeding speeds of 100 wpm is often desired by those that type for pure enjoyment. There's just something about typing really fast and fluently that makes you feel good that only a small amount of people can understand. Despite this being the case, typing more than 100 wpm with 100 percent accuracy is highly beneficial for transcribers, students, office administrators, programmers, online gamers, and more. Even for general computer use you can save so much time and actually enjoy typing.

REDUCE HEALTH RISKS

Avoid developing repetitive strain injury (RSI) with good touch typing habits and eliminate physical and mental fatigue.

MAKE MONEY

Hone your typing skills and become a freelancer on elance or guru. Publishers are looking for people that can write material quickly and accurately. The quicker you can type, the more tasks you can handle which translates to a satisfying income stream.

INCREASE YOUR FINGER DEXTERITY

As you type so fast, you'll be giving your fingers a major workout. With your improved finger dexterity, put it to use if you play guitar or type on your mobile.

WIN COMPETITIONS

It's competitive out there. Typeracer and 10 fast fingers are two examples of games where competition can be high. Finally, you'll be able to be up there on the top of the leaderboard.

DOUBLE YOUR TYPING SPEED

Assuming you type at the average speed of 40 wpm, you could double your speed to 80 wpm with the tips in this guide. You'll be able to type 2x faster than the average person, allowing you to get much more done. 120 wpm (3x faster) is possible as well if you are willing to put in the time.

ANSWER MORE EMAILS

Answering emails is taking up all your time? Answer twice the amount in the same amount of time, freeing up your time for more important tasks.

HAVE FUN

Being able to type fast and fluently is fun! Many typists find their way to websites like Typeracer and 10 fast fingers to type alongside fellow typing enthusiasts. It's a great way to get together and help each push each other to improve speeds in a friendly environment. You never know what you might learn.

BEAT THE DEADLINES
Whether you're a student or employee, impress your boss or teacher by getting your work on before the deadline. Your boss/teacher will be satisfied with you.

BE COMPUTER SAVVY
You will look and feel computer savvy thanks to your ninja typing skills.

THINK OF MORE CREATIVE IDEAS
Type ideas as they come to your head. Because this is much faster than handwriting, you don't risk forgetting them as they come to your head.

IMPROVE YOUR EDITING SKILLS
Make corrections to your work quickly and efficiently. Just like you can put more work on the page in less time, you'll also be able to make more corrections in less time.

HELP OTHERS LEARN
Teach others what you have learnt and let them too experience the joys of being able to type fast. If you have kids that go to school, teaching them to touch type at an early age

will save them so much time throughout their lifetime and encourage them to complete their assignments.

The 7 Keystones For Success

The key to typing fast consists of five core elements. You must pay attention to each one in order to type fast and accurately. I will explain what each keystone is and how it will assist you on your journey to becoming an experienced typist.

1. Set Goals

To become a faster typist, you must set goals. You can increase your typing speed much faster than those who haven't set any goals. In this chapter, I will explain how to set effective goals that motivate you and help you to progress faster.

2. Select The Right Keyboard

There are various types of keyboards and layouts that will affect your typing experience. While your technique is much more important than what keyboard you use, as you improve and/or type more frequently, knowing about alternative keyboard mechanisms and layouts will benefit you in the long run. There is a lot to cover on the topic of keyboards; however, I'll only explain brief concepts and what you need to know without going into technical detail. I'll help you choose the right keyboard for you.

3. Ergonomics

In a typing context, ergonomics is a system that outlines healthy habits to ensure one optimizes their well-being and typing performance. You've probably seen posters in your school or workplace that show a diagram of a human sitting with their back straight and a screen at eye level, telling you the recommended way to sit at a computer. Boring right? Admittedly I break the 'rules' sometimes by slouching in my chair with my feet up on the table when I type, but I wouldn't recommend this! Branches of ergonomics include good posture, muscle tension, eye level, and more. This isn't the most exciting topic in the book so I have kept it short, however, pay attention because it will benefit you in the long-term regarding not just health, but your typing speed as well.

4. Learn To Touch Type

If you're currently using the 'hunt and peck' approach to typing, things need to change. By that I mean, constantly craning your neck up and down between the screen and keyboard to search for the right keys is not the ideal way to type. Every advanced typist understands how painful it is to watch their peers using as little as two fingers, eyes desperately sprawling the keyboard in search for the right key. Imagine being able to double or even triple the speed at which you do now, and not have to look down at the keyboard ever again, because you know exactly where each key is without looking. The high levels of concentration and wasted time using the hunt and peck approach call for a better way, and touch typing is the answer. If you already know how to touch type the chapter is still worth a read to refine your technique and I'm confident you'll learn something new.

5. Eliminate Bad Habits

Bad habits are your worst enemy. The earlier you identify and fix them, the better. Whether you touch type or not, we all pick up bad typing habits. Common ones include bad posture, tense muscles, pushing rather than striking keys, hitting keys with wrong fingers (technically there is no right or wrong finger to use if your sole aim is to type quickly and accurately, however, touch typing has established guidelines for which fingers you should use). More bad habits are often formed when learning to touch type; this guide will notify you of common issues and assist you along the way to avoid them before they become a problem. If you've already learned bad habits, I'll help you identify and fix them.

6. Tips and Techniques

The advanced tips and techniques discussed in this guide are a major factor that sets this apart from others out there. Everyone can learn to touch type and apply good ergonomic practices, but rarely do you find such a large quantity of quality tips that can help you exceed the notorious 100 wpm benchmark. From the ins-and-outs of mechanical keyboard mechanisms to 'striking' instead of 'pushing, there are numerous ways you can hop on the fast track to high speeds. And don't worry: all tips and techniques will be explained without the technical jargon so you can easily understand.

7. Take Action Now

You must take action in order to get the most out of this book. A review of the guide will be compiled so you know exactly what to do at the end of the book, and be on your way to becoming an ultimate typist. I'll also explain the importance of routine and regular practice.

KEYSTONE 1: SET GOALS

In order to type faster (which I presume is why you are reading this book), setting goals are essential. Typing enthusiasts know this. If you ask a typing enthusiast what speed they are aiming for, more often than not they'll be able to tell you. A good goal is a SMART goal. SMART is a mnemonic that explains what makes an effective goal. When creating your typing goal to become a faster typist, read on to find out what makes a SMART goal and then create one that you can work towards.

S: Specific

Your goal should be specific; "I want type faster" is not a specific goal whereas "I want to be able to type at a speed of 90 words per minute" is.

M: Measurable

A goal must be measurable. Can you identify how close you are to achieving your goal? If your goal is "I want to type really fast", how do you know how close you are? If you type at a rate of 50 wpm then you'd most likely consider that 100 wpm is fast, so setting your goal to "I want to be able to type 100 wpm" will give you the ability to track your progress and see how close you are to the end goal.

A: Attainable

You won't achieve your goal if it is unrealistic. If you aim to achieve a speed of 350 words per minute with one-hand behind your back, you'll run into problems. To encourage you to go through with a big goal, set mini-goals. Mini-goals are simply smaller steps along the way. Let's say your goal is to reach an average speed of 90 wpm and you currently type at 65 wpm. Why not set your goal to 70 wpm? It's much easier to reach 70 wpm than it is 90 wpm. Once you hit 70 wpm, increase it to 75 wpm, then 80 wpm, then 85 wpm, and so on. These mini victories will motivate you to keep improving and a way in which many typists have hit the 100 wpm benchmark.

R: Rewarding

How will achieving your goal reward you? By now I'm sure you are aware of how you'll be rewarded otherwise you wouldn't have bought this book. I explained the benefits and rewards in the previous chapter.

T: Time-bound

When do you want to be able to touch type? When do you want to be able to type 80 wpm? When do you want to be able to type 100 wpm? Setting a date of when you want to achieve a goal will motivate you to keep practicing. You'll improve much faster than if you had no time set at all.

What typing speed should I aim to achieve?

If you don't already have a SMART goal because you are struggling, I can offer you some guidance. Take a free online typing test right now so you can see what your typing speed is. If you want to learn to type fast in the shortest amount of time and are struggling to come up with a number, I would recommend aiming for an average speed of 80 wpm. At that rate, you will have...

Doubled the speed of the average person (the average speed is 40 wpm)

Qualified for 99 percent of jobs requiring a set typing speed

Saved twice the amount of time than if you were typing 40 wpm

The most important benefit is the time you save, I cannot stress this enough. It is the reason of all reasons to learn to type fast. Think about this: If you are currently 30 years of age and type at 80 wpm for 2 hours a day 5 days a week until you are 60 years of age, and assuming you type at 40 wpm, you will have saved 325 days of your life. 325 days of your life. If you are younger than 30 or continue typing past the age of 60, even better. Imagine what you could do with all that extra time. Spend more time building your business, bonding with your family and friends and traveling the world. The list is endless. The earlier you learn, the better, but it's never too late. Finally, don't be afraid to aim for higher than 80 wpm, it is just a suggestion! As long as you are prepared to spend more time, speeds such as 100 wpm are very achievable.

KEYSTONE 2: CHOOSE THE RIGHT KEYBOARD

Does the keyboard I type on make a difference?

Yes, but your technique is more important. Don't go out and buy a keyboard thinking you can skimp on your technique and be able to type faster by spending money on an expensive keyboard. As you'll find out in this chapter, the various types of keyboards on the market are huge. I'll break it down so you'll feel confident about choosing the right keyboard.

What types of keyboards are there?

The most common types of keyboards implement certain types of keyboard mechanisms. Rubber-Dome, scissor switch, and mechanical are the three most common. There are others like topre and buckling spring, but these less common types go beyond the scope of this book. 'Keyboard mechanism' is simply a term describing how they keys work when you press them. Each keyboard mechanism gives a different feel, and, therefore, a unique typing experience. I will explain the pros and cons of each and a brief summary of how they work. By the end of this chapter, you'll have a basic understanding of how each keyboard mechanism works and more importantly, which is best for you.

Rubber-dome

Also known as polydomes or membranes, rubber-dome key switching systems are the most common of all. The keyboard you own is most likely rubber-dome because they are the biggest in the market and cheap to make. You have most likely been using these types of keyboards since you first started using a computer.

How do rubber-domes work?

A rubber or silicon sheet with bumps or 'domes' and a cylinder/plunger exists underneath the keycaps. When you press a key, it pushes a cylinder against the dome and the dome makes electrical contact with the circuit board beneath, which is when the computer registers a keystroke. There are other variations of rubber-dome mechanisms but it would be a waste of your time for me to explain the ins and outs of how each one operates (except for scissor-switch technology which you'll learn about next) so I have omitted it from this book. If you'd like to learn more, you can find extra information and links to resources at the end of this book.

Pros and Cons of rubber-domes

Pros:

-They are cheap to buy

-They work

-Easy to clean

Cons:

-They have a 'mushy' feel

-They are less tactile and less responsive

-They don't last as long as other keyboards

-Dust and other things can easily find their way under the keys

Should I use a rubber dome-keyboard?

For the time being, a rubber-dome keyboard is fine. However, if you use a computer frequently and learn to touch type, it is worth discovering the phenomenal advantages of other key switch technologies.

Scissor-switch

Scissor-switches are commonly found in laptop keyboards but are found in some low-profile desktop keyboards too. They closely resemble rubber-dome keyboards but operate in a slightly different manner and have a different feel.

How do scissor-switches work?

They operate similarly to rubber-domes, but instead use a plastic scissor-like mechanism that connects the keycap and cylinder which push on the rubber dome. The result is less 'travel' (how far you have to press the key down) which provides a more tactile feel.

Pros and Cons of scissor-switches

Pros:

-Have a moderate tactile and responsive feel

-Less travel when pressing the key

-Cheaper than mechanical keyboards

-Less likely to get stuff caught under them

Cons:

-More expensive than rubber-dome keyboards

-Harder to clean

What is better: rubber-domes or scissor-switches?

I recommend choosing the one which feels best to you. Many experienced typists I know use laptop keyboards and, therefore, use scissor-switch technology. If you are to use a keyboard over the long term than you wouldn't want to be stuck with a keyboard that feels crap would you? Scissor-switch may cost you an extra few dollars but if it feels better then go for it.

Mechanical Keyboards

Mechanical keyboards are superior. They offer superb durability, instant response, a pleasing tactile feel and come in all kinds of flavors to suit the user's needs. Mechanical switching technology comes in many forms that have specifications tailored for different use. There are various manufacturers such as Cherry, who make Cherry MX switches, and others like Kaihli and other generic brands. Cherry MX is by far the most popular and of the highest quality so will be the focus of this chapter.

How do mechanical keyboards work?

To understand how mechanical keyboards can affect your typing, I'll briefly describe how mechanical keyboards work. They operate similarly to rubber-dome keyboards except they use a spring instead of rubber which results in a more tactile feel and the key returns faster to its original position. Different springs and plunger designs create a different feel which is why MX keys come in all different types (colors) for different purposes.

Pros and Cons of mechanical switches:

Pros:

-Many different types to suit your needs

-Can be tactile

-Responsive

-Have a godlike feel

-More durable so they last longer

-Easy to clean

-Removable keycaps

-Can reduce fatigue

-Heavy

Cons:

-High upfront cost

-Hard to find places to try before you buy

What types of Cherry MX switches are there?

When you are browsing mechanical keyboards online, you'll be presented with many different coloured switches. I'll list below each color and explain their purpose. Take note that 'actuate' means when the computer recognizes that a key has been pressed, and 'tactile' refers to the responsive bump you can feel in some types of switches.

Blue Switches

The consensus among keyboard enthusiasts is that blue switches are the best for typing. They provide tactile feedback, make a clicky sound, and activate actuate when you half-press them. Because they respond halfway through a keypress, it means you'll don't have to spend as much time or effort pressing keys all the way down (bottoming out).

Brown Switches

Browns are similar to blues except they are quieter and softer. They require slightly less force to actuate and have a linear feel with a very slight 'bump' halfway through the keypress. These are the next best recommendation for typing.

Red switches

Reds are often marketed for gamers due to their responsive, smooth linear feel. They are light-weight, quick to actuate and don't make much noise. They can be used for typing. However, if you are new to mechanical keyboards, I wouldn't recommend this unless you prioritize gaming over typing.

Black switches

Blacks are linear switches that require a high force for them to actuate. They are found in point-of-sale stations and occasionally found in gaming keyboards. The advantage is that it's harder to accidentally press them and they rebound faster, but they are likely to cause fatigue when typing. There is a 'super black' variant that can be used for the space bar found on some keyboards with black switches. 'Dark grey' is another one of these variants that require less force than super blacks but more than regular blacks.

Green switches

Greens require an even stronger force than black switches and can be described as a stiff version of blue switches. They can be found in spacebar keys and on some keyboards although much less common than other switches. A variant of these is white switches which are the quieter version of greens.

Clear switches

Clears can be described as the stiff version of browns but are much less common than other switches. They are very tactile and require a strong force to actuate. Grey switches are sometimes used for the space bar. They are noisy and require more actuation force than clears.

Should I upgrade to a mechanical keyboard?

My mind screams yes instantly. You don't need a mechanical keyboard straight away and you may never know the difference until you try. But when you do, you'll wonder why you ever typed on another keyboard. If you use your computer every day and learn to touch type, then I recommend a mechanical keyboard. Although they are costly, they pay for themselves in the long-term. There are cheaper options out there for those with budget in mind. Brands such as Rapoo, Cougar, Razer, Thermaltake, Steelseries, and Tesoro all have budget versions. If your budget is generous than it may be worth taking a look at keyboards crafted by a German manufacturer called DAS. Typing aficionados can be found using these such as Sean Wrona, arguably the most famous typist in the world. He won the Ultimate Typing Championship in 2010 hosted by DAS.

Which coloured switch should I get? There are so many choices!

I'll make this easy for you. If your main purpose is to type fast, efficiently, and comfortably then choose blues or browns. Choose blues if you don't mind noise and have no one around you that would get annoyed by it. Choose browns if you don't like noise and don't want to annoy others around you. If you are interested in trying out mechanical switches before you buy without having to spend a fortune, there are mechanical keyboard switch samplers available online that have up to 8 different coloured keys.

KEYSTONE 3: ERGONOMICS

You may have heard of the boring term before but ergonomics is important for an optimal typing experience and avoiding bad habits. Remember, avoiding bad habits is the one of the five keys to typing really fast so listen up. According to Google, ergonomics is the study of people's efficiency in their working environment. In a typing context, it describes how you can improve your typing experience by modifying your environment and using your body properly. Slouching in your chair and working in a cold room are examples of poor ergonomics. There are hundreds of articles out there on the subject, but I will sum it up for you without an overload of information. The following information is intended for use as a guide only.

1. Good Posture

Good posture is important; not just for health reasons, but for faster typing too. Sit up straight with relaxed shoulders.

2. Relax

As a fluent typist, you must relax your body. A tense body is the bane of an effective typing technique. Ensure you relax your shoulders, arms, wrists, and fingers. Stop and take deep breaths if you feel tense.

3. Feet flat on floor

Your feet should be flat on the floor. You may have to adjust your seat height.

4. Arms and Hands

Your hands should gently rest on the home keys. Your forearms should be in line with your keyboard and elbows comfortably by your side.

5. Adjust Screen and Seat height

The top portion of the screen should ideally line up straight with your eyes. This will help you avoid hunching over and craning your neck, allowing for a more pleasurable typing experience. Adjust your seat height so your feet are flat on the floor.

6. Suitable Environment

What sort of environment are you in? Avoid loud noises that distract you unless you prefer background noise. Discover your ideal temperature. I find in the winter that my hands become cold and stiff, affecting my typing performance. Put the heaters on if you are serious about typing! If it's too hot, then turn on the air conditioner, if you have that privilege.

7. Take regular breaks

Taking regular breaks is important to reduce fatigue. How long you should take a break for is controversial. Some sources say to take a 5-minute break every 30 minutes. Others say to take 'micro breaks' for 1 minute every 10 minutes. If you type for longer periods, I recommend taking a 10-15 minute break every 90 minutes.

8. Do Exercises

Disclaimer: The following exercises are not designed to eliminate existing health issues but may help to prevent developing future ones. If you already have an injury, you should consult a specialist before doing the following exercises. I take no responsibility for the effects that performing these exercises will have on you.

Exercises can help reduce the risk of developing an injury such as RSI (Repetitive Strain Injury). You can perform exercises during your break not just to reduce health risks, but to improve your typing performance too. Personally I don't do these exercises as often as I should but If your fingers are stiff and your body is tense you won't be able to type effectively. Optionally perform the following exercises during a break.

Wrists / Hands / Fingers

Exercise 1: Slowly clench your fists and hold the position for 3 seconds. Reverse the process until your hands are spread out.

Exercise 2: Move your wrists in circles at a moderate pace for 15-20 seconds. Repeat in the opposite direction.

Neck / Shoulders

Exercise 1: Roll your shoulders in circles for 15-20 seconds at a moderate pace. Repeat in the opposite direction.

Exercise 2: Move your shoulders up high and hold for 3 seconds. Bring them down for 3 seconds. Repeat 3 times.

Eyes

Exercise 1: Look at an object in the distance (at least 6 meters away) for 10 seconds. Look back at a closer object. Repeat 3 times.

Exercise 2: Close your eyes for 30 seconds and apply light pressure to the bone around your eyes. Navigate around the bone and do light presses with your fingers. Open your eyes again.

It's easy to forget the importance of good ergonomics. If you feel discomfort, fatigue, pain, or reduced performance, then this may be why. Now that you've made it through this chapter (yay!) we'll move on to the more exciting part of the book.

KEYSTONE 4: LEARN TO TOUCH TYPE

What is touch typing?

Touch typing is the art of typing with all ten fingers without taking your eyes off the screen. Once you learn to touch type, you'll never want to type any other way. Touch typing is the essence of learning to type effectively and efficiently, as fast as possible. You start with your 4 fingers on each hand touching the ASDF and JKL: keys. These are the 'home keys', your default hand positioning on the keyboard. Your fingers return to these keys after striking other keys. The default keyboard layout is the infamous 'QWERTY' which is what I recommend starting out with. 'But I how do I know what keyboard layout I have on my keyboard?' you might ask. Don't worry, 99 percent of keyboards are built with the QWERTY design by default. You'll notice that next to the tab key on the left side of the keyboard is the 'Q' key, followed by 'W', 'E', 'R', 'T', and 'Y'. Later on I'll discuss alternative keyboard layouts and their pros and cons.

How do I learn to touch type?

Online typing tutors are the ideal way to learn how to touch type. I learnt using a program called TypeQuick which took me on a virtual tour around Australia. I typed the letters that appeared on the screen, and it gradually introduced me to new keys throughout the program. I put a cloth over my hands so I couldn't see the keys. It's an extremely effective tool to learn to type which I would highly recommend.

Despite this, it's not fair to you for paying for this book, only to be told to go out and spend more money on products. Fortunately, there are free alternatives in which many others have succeeded in learning to touch type. Ratatype.com is one of those alternatives. Although it won't take you on a virtual journey around Australia like TypeQuick, the fact that it is free and its simplicity makes up for it. Amongst the many other learn-to-touch type sites on the internet, this is my favorite. It has 15 exercises in chronological order that will take you through from the very beginning to the very end until you can touch type. In order to develop muscle-memory in your fingers, I recommend repeating each exercise multiple times rather than moving on to the next step too soon. If you'd rather cruise through the activities, ensure to come back to specific exercises if you are struggling with specific keys. You'll start by learning the home row and gradually progress to learning the upper, bottom, and number row, as well as special keys and punctuation. Ensure you aren't looking down at the keyboard as you learn. Occasionally it is inevitable, but I'd encourage you to put a cloth over your hand. If you're looking down at the keyboard, this is one of the bad habits I've been talking about. I know of touch typists that still look down at the keyboard, and have acknowledged that it is slowing them down dramatically. Before you get jump into typing drills, set a goal for yourself. You may want to type fast, but how fast? Setting goals is important for success which is why I cover the topic in the following chapter.

How long will it take me to learn to type?

The time it takes to learn to touch type varies. Everyone learns at a different pace and the higher the speed you aim for, the more time it will take. There are numerous claims that you can learn to touch type in less than a day. Some sources say it takes 90 minutes, some say it takes 30 days. So which is right? The claims don't mention to what skill-level you'll reach, so neither are right or wrong. You may pick up the absolute basics in a few hours, but you'll have to spend much more time ingraining finger patterns into your muscle memory to develop a profound technique. It will take some patience on your part, but if you dedicate at least 30 minutes a day to typing, you'll learn to type in no time. It's all about getting the finger patterns ingrained into your muscle memory, so you'll end up typing keys automatically. Your body will know where they are without looking because it has done it so many times before.

What speed should I aim for?

What if you want to raise the bar higher than 80 wpm? What if you want to type 100 wpm or even 150 wpm? I can tell you right now, these are not unrealistic goals. Many people have achieved 100 wpm, and few have reached 150 wpm. You can triple the speed of the average person if you aim for 120 wpm. The primary reason expert typists are able to reach these high speeds is simply because they spent more time than others were willing to. Of course, the amount of time spent practicing is not the only factor, but it's a big one. So it begs the question, how much time do you want to spend learning to type faster? As a general rule: The more time you spend learning now, the more time you'll save in the future. The higher the typing speed you aim for, the more time it will take, but the time it takes grows exponentially. To put it simply, look at the following graph.

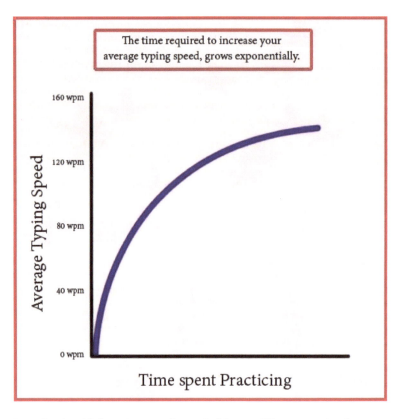

The time required to increase your average typing speed, grows exponentially.

Average Typing Speed

160 wpm

120 wpm

80 wpm

40 wpm

0 wpm

Time spent Practicing

I apologize if the picture above is blurry. The curve in the graph isn't a perfect representation, just a rough idea. You can see that it takes much less time to learn to type at a rate of 80 wpm than 160 wpm. Based on this idea, it's up to you to decide what typing speed you'd like to reach. If you are completely stuck, aim for 80 wpm. When you reach 80 wpm, see how you feel and from there you can decide whether you think it's worth your time improving further.

Keystone 5: Eliminate Bad Habits

In the beginning or over time it is common for people to develop bad habits that negatively affect their typing technique. It's especially important to maintain accuracy by fixing or avoiding certain habits. The list below presents common bad habits to avoid and ways to fix them.

Issue: Stopping when faced with spaces, periods, or commas.

Possible solution: Imagine writing them as part of the preceding or following word.

Issue: Slow finger movements.

Possible solution: Don't worry about typos, keep typing. I'd also recommend relaxing your fingers remember to strike the keys, not push.

Issue: Not using the appropriate finger for some keys.

Possible solution: Although sometimes it's okay to break the 'rules', there may be a character that you could type more fluently if you changed fingers. Experiment.

Issue: Slow reading speed.

Possible solution: Learn to read faster and avoid subvocalizing (speaking the words in your mind) as you type. It's okay to subvocalize when you are learning to touch type, but it may slow you down at higher speeds.

Issue: Getting the order of letters wrong (typing 'thier' instead of 'their', or 'hrose' instead of 'horse')

Possible solution: Practice commonly misspelled words and slow down.

Issue: Poor reading comprehension.

Possible solution: Concentrate. Drink some water to hydrate yourself, sleep for at least 8 hours the night before, and type in an environment with no distractions.

Issue: Pushing the wrong key that is close to the correct one (e.g. 'x' instead of 'z').

Possible solution: Practice typing specific keys with your desired finger. Ratatype.com is a great app for this.

Issue: Sore muscles

Possible solution: Refer to the ergonomics chapter.

KEYSTONE 6: 35 TIPS AND TECHNIQUES

This chapter is highly valuable as it contains a compilation of typing tips that have been gathered from numerous sources such as typing enthusiast forums, books, eBooks, typing aficionados, and myself. Some tips are backed up with quotations from various typists; however, I haven't quoted every single typist that suggested some of these tips on forums; doing so would be tedious and waste your precious time. I've sifted through years' worth of forums on Typeracer.com, 10fastfingers.com (10ff), and many other sources in order to extract the best advice from various typists. The first consists of the 10 most popular tips that are suggested by most typists and the second contains less common tips but not necessarily less effective. Sometimes just applying a few new tips or techniques can make all the difference, especially if you are typing at speeds over 100 wpm. Keep in mind that not every tip will work for everyone so if one doesn't work, try another. After trying some of these out, you'll be surprised how much they can impact your typing performance!

Top 10 Tips

1. Follow the 7 keystones to success.

It's important to follow the 7 keystones I listed earlier in this book as this develops the critical foundation for your typing technique. To jog your memory the 7 keystones are: Ergonomics, Learn to Touch Type, Select the right keyboard, Eliminate Bad Habits, Tips and Techniques, Practice, and Take action now.

2. Focus on accuracy, not speed

Improving your accuracy will improve your speed. A common mistake typists make is trying to type too fast and as a result they make many errors. By constantly making mistakes, you are training your muscle memory to repeat the same mistakes. To improve your accuracy (and therefore your speed) and make less typos, Sean Wrona (one of the fastest typists in the world) suggests that you 'Speed through the easier words and take a little more time on the harder words to ensure accuracy.' It's tempting to ignore this but if you do, it will come back to haunt you and you'll be stuck wondering why you can't improve your typing speed.

3. Read ahead

By reading one word ahead, you'll be prepared for what to type next. As Sean Wrona says, 'Always focus on the word after the word you are currently typing so there are no unnatural pauses in your typing'.

4. Strike keys, don't push

Fast taps are more efficient than mushy presses. Pushing keys with force will wear you out and slow you down. Aim for quick strikes as you type. If you have a mechanical keyboard, this is extra important as you want to avoid bottoming-out the keys unnecessarily. Assuming you have blue or brown switches, the key actuates halfway through the press so you don't need to press it all the way down. At high speeds, this is sometimes inevitable but keep it in mind.

5. Don't look down

If you've developed this bad habit it's hard to break but not impossible. Think of the time you could save and how much faster you could type if you didn't have to look down at the keyboard. When typing or learning to touch type, put a cloth over your hands if you can't resist the urge to look!

6. Play typing games

Typing games are an excellent way to network with other typists and compete in competitions to motivate you. With websites like Typeracer and 10ff, you can compete against others, make new friends, and test your typing speed. I go into more detail about the advantages of typing games later in this book.

7. Practice common letter combinations

As I was sifting through forums a tip that constantly brought itself to my attention was to practice common letter combinations such as 'ough', 'th', 'ing', 'wh', 'tion', 'igh', and 'ea'. You can type your password really fast, can't you? If you practice these letter combinations over and over again, you'll be able to type them as fast as your password. Because they are so common in the English language, you'll be able to fly through words with these combinations.

8. Watch people type faster than you can

This tip is particularly helpful for those stuck around the 100 wpm mark. Watch typists like fyda and reckful on YouTube type over 150 wpm. By watching them, you'll realize that typing at these speeds is possible. If you are typing 100 wpm and they are typing 150 wpm, then surely you can type 110 wpm! This is what goes through my head and I've found it's helped me to break down mental barriers and improve my speed, even when I think I can't go faster.

9. Break the rules

It's rare to find a typist who types perfectly. Not every typist uses the 'right' finger for the 'right' key. I type '1' and 'z' with my ring finger instead of my pinky and 'b' with my right hand instead of my left. Touch typing convention says that this is wrong, however sometimes you just have to break the rules! Sean Wrona says, "I believe my biggest advantage in typing is that I do not necessarily use the same finger to type the same key. I use whichever finger is most comfortable, which can vary based on the context of the letters in the word."

10. Join a forum

Network with other typists. Join a typing forum. There are typists out there that will be willing to help you with any questions you may have. I recommend the Typeracer forum and 10ff forum.

11. Try a Dvorak keyboard layout

The Dvorak keyboard layout has characters placed in different positions on the keyboard. You most likely type on a Qwerty layout so using Dvorak would mean re-learning to type again! Dvorak claims that the layout requires less finger motion, increases typing speed, and decreases more errors compared to Qwerty. The claims are highly controversial and it failed to overcome the popularity of Qwerty despite the study of letter frequencies and physiology that went into it. Dvorak typists are rare although I know of someone who can type 135 wpm with a Dvorak layout and 120 wpm on a Qwerty layout, but this doesn't guarantee you'll be able to type faster with Dvorak. A computer programmer who invented the Workman layout had a bad experience with a Dvorak layout who said, "I didn't like the way Dvorak was laid out especially for the weak fingers of the right hand." This is one of many opinions and a computer programmer uses a keyboard differently compared to the way an author would. Programmers frequently type odd characters and symbols whereas authors are more concerned with letters. No one knows if they'll be able to type faster using Dvorak until they take the time to learn it.

To use Dvorak on Windows 7:

-Click the 'Start' button.

-Click 'Control Panel'

-Click 'Clock, Language, and Region'

-Click 'Change keyboards or other input methods' under 'Region and Language'

-Click 'Keyboards and Languages'

-Click 'Change Keyboards'

-Click 'Add' under the 'General' tab

-Scroll down and click the '+' symbol next to 'English (United States)'

-Click '+' next to 'Keyboard'

-Click the box next to 'United-States Dvorak'

-Click 'Okay'

-Click the menu under 'Default Input Language' and select 'English (United States) - United States-Dvorak

-Click Apply

-In the white box under 'Installed Services' make sure 'United States-Dvorak' is at the top of the list by clicking it and clicking 'Move up'

-To switch between Qwerty and Dvorak, click on the 'Language Bar' tab

-Ensure 'Dock in the taskbar' is selected

-Right click the windows taskbar

-Hover over Toolbars and make sure 'Language bar' is selected

-By clicking on the keyboard icon on the taskbar, you can alternate between Qwerty and Dvorak layouts

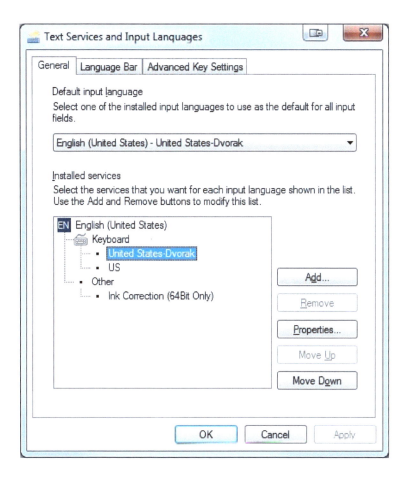

-The window will look like this once you have completed all the steps

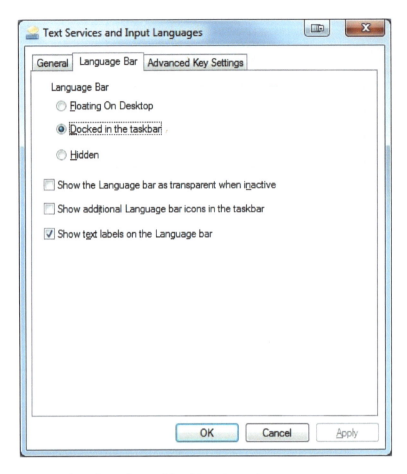

-Ensure 'Dock in the taskbar' is selected

To use Dvorak on Mac OS X:

-Go to 'System Preferences'

-Click on the 'Keyboard' icon

-Click on the 'Input Sources' tab

-Click '+' and select the Dvorak keyboard layout

-Click Add

-Make sure the 'Show input menu in menu bar' option is selected under the 'Input Sources' tab. It will show a flag in the menu bar that shows you which keyboard is in use. To change keyboard layouts, you can click the flag.

12. Try a Colemak keyboard layout

Colemak can be described as a combination of Qwerty and Dvorak layouts which came out in 2006. Colemak claims that your fingers on Qwerty move 2.2x more than on Colemak and 35x more words can be typed using the home row on Colemak compared to Qwerty. There is a small forum where typists post their Colemak experiences. BarneyFifeFan says, "As a professional sermon transcriber, I need to squeeze every umpteenth bit of speed out of my typing. I can honestly say that (once I regain my speed back from my shift from QWERTY) I am going to do way better. I can already feel the reduction in finger movement. Colemak is officially awesome." Another seasoned user named davkol says, "I'm mostly happy with my 80key ErgoDox and Colemak typing experience. It's already good enough efficiency-wise. My hands move less, there are fewer awkward keystroke sequences, and my wrists are relaxed on a split keyboard." No one often knows how much faster or how much they will like an alternative keyboard layout until they try. My recommendation is to stick with Qwerty and try an alternative keyboard layout only if your career involves typing throughout a 9-5 work day. If you would like to try it, you can download the app from the official Colemak website.

13. Try a Workman keyboard layout

The Workman layout was invented by an individual and made its debut in 2010. It was designed to improve on Colemak. It attempts to make common letter combinations easy to type, make backspacing easier, balance the usage required by the left and right hand, reduce the load on your right pinky finger, reduce the amount of travel your fingers must do, and more. The inventor states, "I encourage you to do your own testing and analysis. Note that different keyboard testers will give different results as to what layout is better depending on the criteria that they are using to do their measurements and assessments. Since Workman's philosophy is unique, many testers will register it inferior to others." See the original blog post to learn more and download the layout. Alternatively, TypingStudy.com supports the learning of various keyboard layouts including Dvorak, Colemak, and Workman.

14. Use caps lock if all letters in a word are capitalized

Not all typists hold down shift when typing capital letters when it comes to words that are fully capitalized. For example if you type the word 'PRINCESS', you may find it more efficient to press caps lock with your left pinky finger instead of straining it holding down shift. Sean Wrona says, "I recommend using caps lock instead of shift to type capital letters to allow more flexibility in the hand that you would normally use shift with." I don't recommend caps lock if you only have to type one capital letter in a word, otherwise you have to turn caps lock off which takes two presses, instead of one if you used the shift key.

15. Use keyboard shortcuts

Did you know pressing Ctrl+Backspace (on Windows) backspaces a whole word? You may find this useful because you don't have to tap backspace repeatedly if you make multiple mistakes. Experiment with this to see which way you prefer.

16. Type numbers properly

Don't make the mistake of not learning to type the number row correctly. For years, I avoided the number row and had to look down at the keyboard to type numbers. If you can't type numbers without looking down at the keyboard, it will decrease your speed significantly, especially when you are racing against the clock. Same goes for punctuation. If you play typing games such as Typeracer you'll understand.

17. Know when to use the numeric pad

This tip may contradict the previous tip but sometimes using the numeric pad is faster than using the number row. To clarify, the numeric pad is that set of numbered keys on the right-hand side of most keyboards. This is particularly useful for data entry or when you have to type large clusters of numbers such as phone numbers. Shopkeepers often use the numeric pad to type in various codes, sales data, and passwords.

18. Listen to music

There has been no wide scale study performed to test the effect that music has on typing performance; however, some typists report that music helps them type faster. 10ff user Alethea said, "I started listening to music while typing and I just beat the record on my profile! :3 I had no clue it could make such a huge difference, and I even got a 128 WPM with no misspelled words!". From a rationality perspective, Alethea could be attributing her success to the music when it could be explained by other reasons such as regression to the mean. Excuse me for the technical jargon. Another user named TypeAdom said, "Music is a fantastic aid and can help you enter an accelerate performance state. You'll notice a huge difference from typing with no music and typing with your favorite song on." In a 2003 term paper by Gregory Young, he states, "Appropriately selected musical accompaniment to exercise and sports-related activity may enhance the enjoyment and motivation levels of participants even if it has no impact on their actual performance." Although typing isn't necessarily considered a sports-related activity, it may explain why people feel great when they listen to music while typing. Try it out for yourself! I prefer my favorite songs playing lightly in the background. Anything too loud distracts me and slow music makes me feel like I will type slower.

19. Practice difficult words

When you are typing unfamiliar words, you may find you slow down or make mistakes. Which word would you rather type?, "apple" or "pizazz". If you were like me, you chose "pizazz". Not only is this word unfamiliar, but a Canadian specialist in bioinformatics called Martin Krzwinski, states this word as being one of the most difficult words to type on a Qwerty layout. Other words Krzwinski deemed to be difficult were "piazzas", "pizzas", "suburban", "assuming", "obstinance", and "foramens". Typists on the forum indicate that the words "existentialism", "sovereignty", and "dachshund" are difficult as well. The main point to take away from here is that if you are constantly coming across the same words that you find difficult to type, take note of them and practice them repeatedly. When they come up again, you'll know exactly how to type them.

20. Divide big words into smaller words

By mentally dividing big words into smaller words, you may find it easier to type them. This can often depend on the word. A word I find easier to type by mentally dividing it is "masochistic". I see it as two words, "maso" and "chistic". Over time, you'll find out what words you struggle with so try this technique to type them with confidence.

21. Expand your vocabulary

By learning new words, you will be able to type faster. Unfamiliar words are hard to type and often cause unnatural pauses while you're 'in the zone'. If you become familiar with them and practice typing them over and over again, you won't have issues in the future. Personally I'm a fan of Vocabulary.com where you can make your own lists of words to learn.

22. Start typing at a young age

If you started typing at a young age, you are at an advantage. "But I'm old!" Don't worry, it's never too late to learn to type fast. Just know that the earlier you start, the more time you will have to improve.

23. Type in a different language

Typing in a different language such as Spanish or German will improve your muscle memory by learning uncommon letter combinations. I suggest these two languages because they closely resemble English and you'll be able to type most of the words with your keyboard. Other languages require a special keyboard with special characters such as Greek. 10ff hosts competitions where you can type words from various languages. Typeracer also allows you to select a different language under the 'More options' menu on the home page. 10ff user chupachupsa said he found TypingStudy.com very useful as well. The site is neatly laid out and immediately presents you with a wide range of languages to choose from.

24. Type text backwards

Much like typing in a different language, typing paragraphs backwards is a great way to ingrain odd letter combinations into muscle memory. When odd combinations do come up, you'll know how to type them fluently. 10ff user cameron23 says, "I heard typing a book backwards will be a surefire way of increasing your WPM."

25. Type in the morning

If you have a choice to type in the morning instead of later in the day, do it. Studies show that you are most productive in the first 2.5-4 hours of your day. Have a sip of coffee if you need to wake yourself up.

26. Play the piano or guitar

There have been reports of piano players that naturally pick up typing as a skill. A fellow typing enthusiast told me they he was a pianist (piano player) and learnt to type naturally. At this time of writing, he consistently averages over 130 wpm. There are no scientific studies to confirm this, but it makes sense if you think about it. Both typists and pianists develop excellent finger dexterity and coordination.

27. Use F.lux to make text easier to read

F.lux is an app for your computer that you can download for free. It aims to match the colors of your computer screen to your environment depending on the time of the day. This is especially handy if you type at night. Relieve your eyes and eliminate that burning white glow from your computer screen.

28. Adjust your monitor

Make it easier to read text as you type by angling your monitor away from lights and windows. You can also manually adjust the brightness and contrast to your desired setting (most monitors will have buttons at the bottom that you can press). High contrast mode is another option which makes text easier to see, especially in dark settings.

To enable high contrast mode in Windows 7:

-Click the 'Start' button

-Click "Control Panel"

-Click "Ease of Access"

-Click "Ease of Access Center"

-Click "Make the computer easier to see"

-You'll be given various options that you can experiment with. To enable high contrast mode just click the box that says "Turn on or off High Contrast when left ALT + left SHIFT + PRINT SCREEN is pressed"

-Press left ALT + left SHIFT + PRINT SCREEN

29. Improve room lighting

If you are typing at your computer frequently, poor lighting can cause numerous issues such as eye irritation, difficulty seeing the screen, and headaches.

To improve the lighting in your environment:

-Diffuse overhead lighting with filters

-Reduce the intensity of overhead lights

-The recommended amount of light in office should be between 300 and 500 lux

30. If you make a mistake, just keep typing

It's tempting to correct yourself when you've made a mistake, but often it's best to just keep typing. Some typing apps won't let you keep typing without correcting your mistake which is good when you are learning to touch type, but once you've refined your technique you should keep typing. Stopping to correct mistakes will significantly reduce your typing speed. I say this with caution because I don't want to confuse you. If you are making more than 5 mistakes per minute, you should slow down and work on your accuracy. Learning to type accurately will ensure you don't make too many mistakes in the first place. If you are making less than 5 mistakes per minute, keep typing. It's not uncommon for experienced typists to make a few natural mistakes every now and then.

31. Practice typing the 1,000 most common English words

10ff has a feature ('Top 1000) that allows you to practice typing the 1,000 most common words in the English language. It also has a hardcore mode if you want to challenge yourself. The more words you master, the faster you'll be able to type.

32. Regularly ask yourself what is slowing you down

10ff user jolos suggests every month you ask yourself why you aren't typing faster than last month, and if not, why?

33. Review your goals

Don't lose track of your goal. Goal setting and mini-goals were discussed earlier in this book. Review your goal to see how you are doing.

34. Use autocorrect in Microsoft Word

If you are typing documents in Microsoft Word, you can save a significant amount of time by automatically converting short phrases to words with the autocorrect feature. For example, when you type 'autom', you can set autocorrect to change it to 'automatically'. By doing this, you are typing half the amount you need to. Imagine the time you could save! If you find yourself typing big words repeatedly, this is a solution so you can type more in less time.

To access autocorrect options in Microsoft Word:

-Click on 'File' in the top-left hand corner

-Click 'Options'

-Click 'Proofing'

-Click 'AutoCorrect Options...'

-Type the word you want to be replaced in the 'Replace:' box. For example, 'hippo'

-Type the other word you want it to be replaced with. For example, 'hippopotamus'

-Click 'Add'

-Now when you type 'hippo', it will automatically convert into 'hippopotamus'

To access autocorrect options in other versions of Microsoft Word:

-Click the 'Menus' tab

-Click the 'Tools' menu

-Click 'AutoCorrect Options...'

-Follow steps 5-8 in the previous instructions

35. Convert your voice to text

If you want a break from typing, speech recognition software has come a long way and allows you to type with your voice. Dragon NaturallySpeaking is by far the most refined dictation software out there. The average human speaks at a rate of 120-150 wpm so you could type 7,200 - 9,000 words in an hour by speaking. Additional features allow you to open applications and practically control your computer which may come in handy on those days where you simply can't type.

KEYSTONE 7: TAKE ACTION NOW

It's time to put your newly acquired knowledge to use. You'll get the most out of this book by taking action on what you've learnt. Below are the steps to master the art of typing.

-Set your SMART goal

-Choose a keyboard

-Practice good ergonomics

-Learn to touch type

-Identify and fix bad habits

-Review the 35 tips chapter and try some out

-Practice for at least 30 minutes every day, 5 days per week

Practice

A last note on practice. "Practice" is the most common tip you'll get from expert typists. No expert typist reached 150 wpm without sufficient hours spent typing. However, there is more to it than just practice. Ensure practice is good practice. Good practice involves practicing good habits, whereas bad practice involves practicing bad habits.

Resources

There are various online resources which are both fun and aim to improve your typing skills. All of the resources listed are completely free and been hand-picked amongst hundreds of others, as the ones with an excellent reputation and regular users.

Typing Tutors

Ratatype

Amongst the many other learn-to-touch type sites on the internet, Ratatype stands out as being easy to get started and very simple to follow. It has 11 exercises in chronological order that will take you through from the very beginning to the very end until you can touch type. In order to develop muscle memory in your fingers, I recommend repeating each exercise twice rather than moving on to the next step so soon.

Keybr

Keybr is another well-known typing tutor. It will guide you step-by-step based on your skill level and will record your statistics if you make an account. Try not to look at keyboard on the screen too often!

Typing Games

Typeracer

Typeracer is a free online typing game that connects typists worldwide where players race each other by typing (often insightful) quotes. It was the first multiplayer typing game created and possibly the most popular. As they type, each player has a vehicle on the screen that races towards the finish line. The game allows typists of all abilities to connect with each other and improve their typing speed. It is also home to the best typists in the world, those that reach speeds of up to 200 wpm. By registering for an account, you can customize your profile and track your progress. Statistics will be created based on how well you do in each race. You can track your average speed, max speed, number of races won/completed, skill level, experience level, and rank. A visual representation that is updated after each race will help you keep track of your goals and monitor your progress. Practice modes are available and the ability to create private rooms where you can invite your friends. You can message other typists, participate in the forum, or even make yourself known on the public leaderboard if you type fast enough. Fellow racers will be happy to help you on the forum with any questions you may have. There are numerous themes available to users that can enhance your typing experience on the site. A highly renowned one is the eye-friendly theme for Typeracer. Its primary function is reducing the stress on eyes, giving it a dark theme and a nifty racing flag behind the typewriter logo.

10 Fast Fingers

10 Fast Fingers is one of the most popular typing resources for both novice and experienced typists. The program gives

you one minute to type as many words as you can. The words are often simple and you are allowed to make mistakes which you can't do on Typeracer. There are both test and competition modes. Test mode is a simple one-minute typing test whereas competition mode is where multiple typists compete by typing the same texts within a 24-hour period, and you gain a ranking depending on how fast you typed. Achievements are another great feature that will motivate you to improve.

Typing Maniac

Typing maniac is the most popular typing game on Facebook. Words fall from the top of the screen at various rates, and your job is to type the words before the hit the bottom. The most exciting part is typing the words that give you power-ups and special bonuses, such as typing 'ice' which freezes all the words. Share your score and invite your friends to play (or don't, let's be honest - nobody likes Facebook game invites).

Fowl Words

Fowl words is a fun game where you are given 7 random letters and out of those letters you have to type words that you can make with the letters given. Each level it gets harder. I mention this game because it is a nice break from time limits. You can relax and enjoy guessing words. Additionally, the faster you can type, the more words you can get than the average person.

Nitro Type

Nitro type is similar to Typeracer. You race against other players, but you have special abilities achievements to unlock. It's less popular than Typeracer and 10 fast fingers but worth checking out.

<u>Typing Tests</u>

TypingTest.com

Not only does Typingtest.com appear as the first result in Google after typing in 'typing test', but it's one of the most popular. You are given a choice of various texts of which to type for 1-5 minute(s). At the end, it will show your typing speed and accuracy.

Typing Zone

Players from different countries compete in various typing tests, and their scores are shown on a leaderboard that can be filtered by ranking or country. One feature that attracts typists is the alphabet race: see how fast you can type the alphabet. The current record holder, Christophe Jousselin from France, typed the alphabet in 0.941 seconds. Others include typing the alphabet backwards, texts in different languages, and typing Pi to 200 digits.

<u>Typing Forums</u>

TypeGood Facebook Page

A great space to share your typing progress with others and keep up to date with tips and reminders to improve your typing skills.

Typeracer Forum

Feel free to ask any question about Typeracer or typing in general.

10 Fast Fingers Forum

Another great forum to ask any question about typing or about the site.

Colemak Forum

A forum where you are likely to find typing enthusiasts that like to experiment with Dvorak, Colemak, and other unique keyboard layouts.

Workman Forum

Discuss the workman keyboard layout here.

Bonus: 10 Frequently Asked Questions

What is an average typing speed?

40 words per minute.

Is 100 wpm good for a 14-year-old?

That's a fantastic speed! 100 wpm is a brilliant speed no matter what your age but the younger you are, the better because you'll save time throughout your life. Considering the average speed is 40 wpm, if you are typing at 60 wpm, you are already saving 50% more time. Don't worry too much about your age, just focus on reaching your goals.

What are the hardest English words to type?

Different people find different words hard to type; however, it's common for words to be difficult if they have too many characters next to each other, repeated characters, or unfamiliar words. A list of words that you may find difficult to type are... "pizazz", "pizzas", "obstinance", "existentialism", "sovereignty", and "dachshund". What words do you find hardest?

Who is the fastest typist in the world?

There are numerous claims to be the fastest typist in the world, as well as cheaters that have false records to shown on various typing websites. Most people agree that Sean Wrona is genuinely the fastest typist in the world. He won the Ultimate Typing Championship in 2010. He can type in short bursts of over 200 wpm and longer bursts around 170-180 wpm. Other honorable mentions are Barbara Blackburn, who is deemed the Guinness World Record Holder and peaked at 212 wpm and maintained a speed of 150 wpm for 50 minutes.

How is typing speed measured?

It is measured according to the amount of words typed in 1 minute and expressed as 'wpm' (words per minute). A word is considered to be 5 characters/keystrokes long. "Black" and "B ack" are considered the same length because they both consist of 5 keystrokes including the space. "Black Cats" would be considered 2 words because it requires 10 keystrokes to type.

Will a different keyboard really increase my typing speed?

You won't know until you try. Some keyboards should theoretically increase your speed such as a mechanical keyboard with blue switches because the keys require less effort and less travel distance to actuate.

How long will it take me to reach 100 wpm?

The time it takes is different for everyone, but you'll certainly reach 100 wpm much faster than someone who has not followed the keystones in this guide. The time it takes to achieve certain speeds is explained in the touch typing chapter.

How can some people type 200 wpm?

These typing enthusiasts have been practicing and refining their technique for years. The speeds are often reached in short bursts of no more than 1 minute. A study was performed by a group of German psychologists in the 1990's on the amount of time violinists had practiced to get reach their current level of skill. The results concluded that it takes 10,000 hours of practice to achieve mastery in a field. So if you want to type 200 wpm, you better get typing!

How long will it take me to learn to touch type?

It's hard to put a number on this because it's different for everyone. Between a week and a month is an estimation but all depends on the person and how regularly you practice.

What is N-Key Rollover (NKRO)?

When a key is pressed on your keyboard, your computer will register it as a keystroke regardless of how many other keys are being pressed down at the same time. Some keyboard manufacturers refer to this as 'anti-ghosting'. Despite the marketing hype, it's not that relevant to typing. By default, keyboards will be able to register a max of 10 simultaneous keys and 4 modifier keys such as Ctrl, Shift, Alt, and Caps Lock.

BONUS: MAKE MONEY BY TYPING

As you know by now, the list of benefits you can obtain is plentiful. I'd now like to mention in what activities and occupations touch typing will be of use. I've included 10 hand-picked occupations and activities in which typing will help you perform at your best and enhance your employability prospects. If you are thinking about getting a job that involves typing, that's great as many employers these days won't consider you for a position if you cannot type fluently. Some firms hiring audio typists (transcriptionists) require you to have an average typing speed of 70 words per minute, almost double the typing speed of a novice. Although that may sound difficult to reach, if you read and follow the keystones to success in this guide, you'll be fine. If you already have a job in the following list, you are probably already aware of why it's so beneficial. Even if you don't have or intend to get a job at this stage, typing will improve your workflow with hobbies such as online gaming and writing. Read on to find out what jobs are available to you as a typist

1. Office administrators

Office admins contribute to the success of an organization through a variety of tasks that include but are not limited to: organizing documents, writing letters, word processing, making phone calls, and more. Since much of their time can be spent typing, it pays to have touch typing skills. Impress your employer by completing tasks fast; he/she might even give you a raise.

2. Writers

Do you write books? Blogs? Whatever you write, being able to type fast and accurately will help you get more done in less time, allowing you time to spend time elsewhere, like with your family or playing online games, whatever you fancy.

3. Editors

As an editor, you know it's frustrating having to constantly change your focal point between the keyboard and screen. Learn to touch type and eliminate this annoyance forever.

4. Online Gamers

"Playing video games is not a job!" you might say, however, believe it or not, online gaming is huge these days. It is under constant growth, and more gamers are emerging with more wealth under their belts. One such platform in which online gamers acquire wealth is Twitch TV, a live streaming website owned by Facebook Inc. where people play games. Online gamers may find that their typing skills help them navigate the keyboard more quickly and accurately when playing games that require keyboard input. Touch typing teaches you the positions of each key on the keyboard so when you require a certain key in a game, you won't have to spend critical time looking for it.

5. Computer programmers

Get more lines of code done in less time. Coding is a common skill required by employees today so outshine your competitors by being more efficient.

6. Journalists

Typing is great for journalists because it gives you the ability to take more notes at a faster rate, making sure you absorb crucial information that you otherwise may have missed. If you record audio on a microphone, you'll be able to transcribe it later with your typing skills.

7. Students

Students who can type fast impress their peers and get assignments done faster. If you're one to leave an assignment to the last minute, typing skills will come in handy. Your friends may even hire you to type their assignments for them!

8. Paralegals

As a paralegal (legal assistant) you are likely to be found typing up legal documents. Put your typing skills to good use.

9. Transcriptionists

Transcriptionists convert audio recordings into a written record. Along with literacy skills and a sound understanding of the associated terminology, you can start transcribing today as a freelancer if you will.

10. Data Entry

Data entry jobs involve the entering data into electronic databases and as a result, many employers will require a minimum average typing speed for you to be considered for a job. The type of work varies among companies. For example, if you worked for a sales company, it'd be likely that you will enter sales data and client information into databases.

11. Earn money at home by becoming a freelancer

Start by getting on Elance or Guru now and promote your typing skills as a service to others and get paid for it. An additional pathway is that of Fiverr.com, where people will buy your services upwards of $5.00. It doesn't sound like much, but Fiverr has grown in popularity and you can add additional services to earn you more. If this is something you're interested, be sure to check out the website and show people your typing prowess, as well as any other skills you have on offer.

Bonus: How I Went From 0 to 125 wpm and You Can Too

I began typing at the age of 8 while I was at school in 2003. My teacher set aside lessons for the class to type 2-3 times a week. He made us put a cloth over our hands so we couldn't see the keys, although every now and then I had a peak underneath! This was excellent discipline and taught me to touch type without having to look down at the keyboard. Our class typed on a program called TypeQuick which included a Koala that travels around Australia we typed. The koala taught us how to touch-type through interactive activities. We were rewarded with candy if we got a good speed and accuracy. As I improved, I looked to online typing games and came across Typeracer. I signed up in 2009 and fell in love. The majority of my training hours were spent on Typeracer. As an online gamer, I often spent time communicating with other players by typing. Games I played that required me to type were Runescape and World of Warcraft. This was a passive method of practice which boosted my typing speed over the years. I developed bad habits along the way, such as not using the right-shift key and avoiding the number row where possible. To exceed 100 wpm, it helped me to be inspired by watching others type faster than I could. Some YouTube searches lead me to typists like Fyda, Sean Wrona, and Reckful. Watching them gave me that mental boost which I believe helped me break a mental barrier and up my typing speed with more practice. I have had so much practice that my hands flow from key to key. With years of passive practice (by 'passive' I mean learning as I go along without thinking about it) I was able to exceed 100 wpm. To hit 125 wpm required tweaking my technique by re-learning to type the number row, relaxing, eliminating bad habits, upgrading to a mechanical keyboard, setting goals, and typing with typists on my level. Occasionally I can type 150 wpm and you can too if you follow the advice in the guide. Put the 7 keystones to success into action and you'll be on your way to becoming a super-fast typist.

FINAL MESSAGE

Thank you for reading! If you found this book useful I'd highly appreciate it if you left a short review on Amazon. Your support makes a huge difference and I read all reviews so I can take your feedback and make this book even better.

Have a great day and happy typing!

www.ingramcontent.com/pod-product-compliance
Lightning Source LLC
Chambersburg PA
CBHW041144050326

40689CB00001B/477